Scatterbrain

by Joan Nichols • illustrated by Mark Weber

PEARSON
Scott
Foresman

Editorial Offices: Glenview, Illinois • Parsippany, New Jersey • New York, New York
Sales Offices: Needham, Massachusetts • Duluth, Georgia • Glenview, Illinois
Coppell, Texas • Ontario, California • Mesa, Arizona

Every effort has been made to secure permission and provide appropriate credit for photographic material. The publisher deeply regrets any omission and pledges to correct errors called to its attention in subsequent editions.

Unless otherwise acknowledged, all photographs are the property of Scott Foresman, a division of Pearson Education.

Illustrations by Mark Weber

Photograph 24 Getty Images

ISBN: 0-328-13632-8

3 4 5 6 7 8 9 10 V0G1 14 13 12 11 10 09 08 07 06

I'm late. I'm late. The words beat in Jenna's head as she rode her bicycle out of Central Park, dismounted, waited impatiently for the light to change, and then walked it quickly across the street. She hurried into her apartment building and onto the elevator. It was six-thirty, and she had promised she would be back by six.

She'd been with Rosa and Joanne, her best friends from elementary school, and they had lost track of the time. On Monday, all three would be starting different middle schools. They wouldn't see much of each other from then on, and Jenna had wanted to spend some time with them.

As the elevator door groaned open, Jenna pushed her bike through and ran down the hall to her apartment. Her mother was in the kitchen, stirring something in a bowl.

"Jenna, where were you? You're a half-hour late. Let me have the eggs so I can finish making this cake."

The eggs! Jenna had completely forgotten the eggs! She had promised to buy them at the grocery store on her way home so her mother could bake a cake for her father's birthday the next day.

"Did you remember to buy the eggs?"

Jenna winced at the distressed look on her mother's face. "I'll go now," she said softly.

"Never mind." Her mother sighed. "Your father will be home any second. We have a Girl Scout meeting to attend with Jolie right after dinner." Jolie was Jenna's eight-year-old sister. "I'll have to finish the cake tomorrow." She sighed again. "If only you weren't such a scatterbrain."

Scatterbrain. Jenna washed up for dinner, the word burning in her mind. She meant to keep her promises, to do what she said she would do. But all too often she forgot. Notes from school didn't reach her parents, or homework assignments didn't make it home. She was often late for supper, and in the winter, her mittens were always left behind.

How was she going to handle middle school? Instead of the one in her school district on Manhattan's Upper West Side, she would be going to a specialized school for students who loved science. The one time she had been there it had seemed big and confusing: there were lots of different classes and different teachers.

The school was near Gramercy Park. Like a lot of New Yorkers, Jenna measured distance in blocks, not miles. Her new school was about eighty blocks south and four blocks east of where she lived.

At least she didn't have to worry about getting there. Jenna's mother was too nervous to let her ride the train by herself, so she and her mother rode the subway together. They had worked out a routine.

After dropping Jolie off at her school, they walked to the subway station at 96th Street and Central Park West and took the C train to 14th Street. Here they changed for the Brooklyn-bound L train and got off at the Third Avenue stop. From there it was a few blocks to Jenna's school. It was just a few blocks farther to the publishing company where her mother worked as an editor.

By the end of the first week, Jenna felt like an old pro. At the Third Avenue station she confidently pulled her new MetroCard out of her backpack, swiped it through the card reader, and pushed through the turnstile.

The card, which was free for the school's students, was hers for the school year. The school had handed them out on the first day. It paid for her transportation to and from school every day.

The teacher who handed out the cards told the students to write down the number on the back and keep it in a safe place. Having the number would make it easier to replace the card if it was ever lost or stolen. Jenna planned to write the number in her diary at home, although she hadn't gotten around to it yet.

On one trip home during the second week of school, Jenna told her mother all about her new school. "Most of my teachers are great," Jenna chattered to her mother as they clutched a pole. "I love science class. Gym isn't as hard as I thought it would be. And today I signed up to work on the school newspaper."

This meant at least one day a week Jenna would have a fun thing to do after school, instead of sitting in the auditorium while she waited for her mom to pick her up.

"Best of all, Mom, I've made a friend. Her name is Suzanne and she's on the newspaper staff too." Making friends had been hard. Lots of kids came from the same elementary schools, so they knew each other. She and Suzanne had liked each other right away. They had both come from other schools and didn't know many kids.

"Look, there she is now!" A girl Jenna's age was waving frantically and squeezing her way through the crowded car.

"Hi, Jenna. I didn't know you took this train," said Suzanne.

Jenna introduced Suzanne to her mother, who said, "I'm afraid we have to get off at the next station and change for the uptown C train."

Suzanne laughed. "That's OK. So do I."

"You do?" Jenna exclaimed. They hurried through the station. "How far do you have to go?"

"To 86th Street," Suzanne replied.

"That's just one stop before me," said Jenna. The C train was already waiting at the station. They managed to jump on just before the doors closed. "How come this is the first time I've seen you?" Jenna asked.

"My dad drives me in the morning. But I'm on this train every day around this time."

"By yourself?" Jenna's mother asked.

"Sure. My dad and I practiced all summer. He taught me to notice the signs so I always get on and off the right trains at the right stops. I also figured out what to do in an emergency. I have my dad's number programmed in my cell phone. I check in with him along the way."

"Your dad must really trust you," said Jenna's mother.

"Yeah," said Suzanne. "It took me a little while to learn the route, but now I've got it down cold."

"Of course," Suzanne added, "it would be more fun if I had someone else to travel with." She winked at Jenna. "Know what I mean?"

"Oh, Mom, could I? Please?" It would be so wonderful to ride the train with Suzanne. Jenna wouldn't have to spend part of the afternoon in a noisy auditorium, and she could become better friends with Suzanne. They could talk all the way home.

Jenna's mother frowned. "Well, I'm not sure." She looked at Suzanne. "I'll have to talk about it with your father."

Suzanne added, "Don't worry! I could help Jenna learn how to do it."

Jenna felt her face burn. Her mother was still frowning. She wouldn't say anything to embarrass Jenna in front of her friend, but Jenna knew what she was thinking: *scatterbrain*. Jenna's heart sank. How could she convince her mother that she could be as sensible and trustworthy as Suzanne?

The train pulled into 86th Street. Suzanne waved and got off. "See you Monday, Jenna," she said.

Jenna said, "Mom, could we practice like Suzanne and her father? I'd pretend I was on my own, but you'd be there to make sure that I didn't make mistakes. When you see that I know what I'm doing, you could let me ride the subway home with Suzanne."

Her mother didn't answer until they left the subway and were walking to pick up Jolie from her after-school program. "I'm willing to give the practicing part a try, Jenna, but I really do need to discuss this with your father. Then we can both decide when you're ready to come home with Suzanne."

Her mother didn't add *if ever*, but Jenna knew she was thinking it. She promised herself that she would prove she was reliable, no matter how long it took. She would try as hard as she could. Jenna vowed that she wouldn't be a scatterbrain anymore!

For the next two weeks Jenna worked hard. She got a copy of the subway map to study. She learned about the different trains that stopped in the stations she used and where they went.

She and her mother pretended they didn't know each other when they rode the train. It was like they were playing secret agents, and it was fun. In no time, Jenna was getting on and off the trains at each station with such ease that she didn't need her mother there at all.

She was less scatterbrained in other ways too. She copied all her homework assignments and brought them home, and she was even on time for meals.

On the following Monday afternoon, as Jenna waited in the auditorium for her mother, she decided that tonight she would ask her parents for permission to ride home alone on the train with Suzanne.

It was time. She knew she could do it. She knew what to do, but right now, she needed to find her math assignment.

Angrily, Jenna searched through her backpack.
She was sure she had put it in the back compartment.
She turned the backpack upside down and shook it
vigorously. A waterfall of papers landed on the floor.

Hidden under a notebook was her math assignment.
Jenna squashed the rest of the papers and books back
into her pack and settled down to start her homework.

At five-thirty her mother arrived. She looked frazzled
and distracted. "I'm so tired," she said. "My work at the
office is really piling up."

"Think about how much time it would save if you didn't have to pick me up from school every day," Jenna said.

"Oh, Jenna, not now. We can talk about it some other night," her mother sighed.

"Really, Mom, you know I can do it. All this week I've traveled by myself with you just following along to watch. You didn't have to tell me what to do at all." She looked at her mother with pleading eyes. "So don't you think I'm ready to go home in the afternoons with Suzanne?"

Her mother smiled. "You have been more responsible lately. Not just in riding the subway, but with other things too. I'll talk to your father tonight. We will come to a decision together."

"Yes!" Jenna cheered. She took this as a good sign. If her parents talked about it, there was a good chance they would say "yes."

They walked down the steps of the Third Avenue station. Jenna reached around to the front pocket of her backpack for her MetroCard. But her fingers did not feel the familiar thin plastic card.

"Just a minute, Mom," she called out as her mother headed for the turnstile. "I'm still looking for my card."

Jenna pulled the backpack around in front of her. Her fingers explored the pocket again. It was empty. How could that be? She remembered dumping out her papers to find her math homework; she must have thrown the card in with her other stuff. She squatted down and unzipped her pack. People raced around her on their way to the train.

"Hurry, Jenna. The train's coming," Mom said.

"I know my MetroCard is in here somewhere." Jenna could feel her mother watching her. Her fingers moved faster, searching for the missing card.

The train roared into the station. The doors slid open. Passengers pushed their way on and off. The doors slid shut, and the train roared off. Jenna continued to pull papers out of her backpack.

Her mother said, "I can't wait any longer. I'll buy you a one-way fare card now and you can look in your backpack when we get home."

Jenna could sense her mother's silent disapproval the whole ride home. The card had to be somewhere in her backpack. It just had to be.

But it wasn't. After dinner that night, Jenna and her parents had a talk. Not about riding the subway with Suzanne, but about Jenna's lost card. "But surely you wrote down the card number," her father said.

"I meant to," she said miserably. "But I forgot."

Her father shook his head. "You're a bright girl, Jenna. Your mother and I were very proud that you could fulfill the requirements to get into the special science school."

"We want you to be happy there—to learn and flourish," her mother continued.

"We don't want to worry all the time that you will do something foolish or forget something important. Do you understand?" her father asked.

"Yes, Dad," Jenna said, hanging her head.

"Without the number, it will take a while for the school to replace your student MetroCard," her mother said. "I'll buy you a card for now. You'll repay me from your allowance. Is that understood?"

"Yes, Mom," said Jenna.

At lunch the next day, Jenna sat with Suzanne in the cafeteria. Jenna told her about the lost card and what her parents had said. "You're so sensible and reliable," Jenna said. "I don't know how you do it. I'm such a scatterbrain."

Suzanne laughed. "I used to be worse than you. If my mom sent me to the store to buy a newspaper I'd come back with a loaf of bread. That is, if I remembered to bring anything back at all!"

"Really?" Jenna was amazed to hear this. "How did you change?"

"It was something my mom told me," replied Suzanne.

"What was it?"

"She told me to think of the traffic light."

"The traffic light? What does that mean?"

"I'll show you." Suzanne pulled out her pen. "I have some labels in my backpack." On a blank label, she drew a traffic light with three lights. Next to them she wrote STOP, THINK, GO. "My mom said being scatterbrained usually means not paying attention when you need to. So she drew this picture on a label and told me to stick it where I'd always see it. I put it on the back of my hand."

"And it worked?" Jenna asked.

"It took awhile, but it worked. It reminded me whenever I was about to do something in a rush to *stop, think* about what I was doing or needed to do, and then *go* ahead. Pretty soon I didn't have to wear the sticker anymore. The traffic light flashes in my brain whenever I need it," Suzanne explained.

"Do you think that would work for me?" asked Jenna.

"Try it and see. Stick it where you know you will be able to see it," said Suzanne.

Jenna decided to wear her traffic light stuck to the inner part of her arm. That way she could see it easily but other people couldn't.

She wasn't ready to explain why she needed it. That would only embarrass her.

As Jenna settled herself in the auditorium that afternoon, her cell phone rang. It wasn't supposed to be on in school, but she'd forgotten to turn it off.

For once, being scatterbrained paid off. It was her mother, and she sounded worried. "I'm glad I reached you," she said. "Jolie's school called. Jolie was running a fever. I had to bring her home. Now she's in bed, feeling better, but I can't leave her to come get you. Maybe I can find a neighbor who'll watch her for an hour—"

Jenna interrupted. "Mom, it's OK. I can get home by myself. You know I can."

"No, Jenna. I'm sure I can find someone if you just give me a few minutes."

"Mom, please," Jenna pleaded. "I really can do it."

"Well," her mother hesitated.

"I'll try and catch up with Suzanne. But if I don't I'll be all right. I have my cell phone. I'll call you if there are any problems," Jenna said.

"Well, I suppose it's all right," her mother said. "Leave your phone on. I'll keep in touch."

Jenna packed up her things and looked for Suzanne, but she was nowhere to be seen. She must have left already.

Jenna walked down the street feeling strong and confident. At last, she was getting a chance to prove what she could do. She rode the L train to the last stop, got off, and walked up then down the stairs to the uptown C train.

The platform was crowded. People milled about, looking annoyed. The loudspeaker squawked, but Jenna ignored it. It was usually just a reminder not to stand close to the edge. An E train pulled in, but it was headed for Queens, not uptown.

An A train pulled in on the other platform, and almost everyone boarded it. But Jenna knew that although the A train went uptown, it was an express. It didn't stop at 96th Street.

The C train should be next, Jenna thought.

Instead, after a long wait, another E train pulled in, then another A. What was going on? Where was the C train?

The loudspeaker squawked again. Jenna lifted her hands to cover her ears and saw the traffic light label stuck to her arm. STOP. THINK. Was there something she should be paying attention to? Maybe she needed to listen to the loudspeaker? She listened carefully. "Due to an accident at West 4th Street, C train service has been suspended. The A train will be making all local stops to 59th Street," the loudspeaker stated.

That's why everyone got on the A train! What about local stops after 59th Street? Her parents' most important rule was not to talk to strangers, so she couldn't ask anyone except a conductor, but none were around.

Maybe I should call my mom, Jenna thought. But when she pulled her cell phone out of her backpack, she saw that it wasn't working. The batteries were dead.

Now what? Panic bubbles rose inside her. STOP. THINK. A glance at her stoplight picture calmed her down. She had her subway map in her backpack, didn't she? She had learned how to read it, hadn't she? Jenna pulled out her map and looked for her stop.

Yes, there was her stop, 96th Street. The A train did not stop there. Well, she knew that. But the B train did.

Of course! She'd seen that train stop there many times. But where could she get the B train? She ran her finger down the blue line on the map to 59th Street. The A train stopped at 59th Street, and so did the B train.

Jenna put her map in her backpack and stepped onto the A train that had just pulled in. Her parents would not be happy that she had forgotten to recharge her cell phone. But Jenna had figured out a way to get home on her own. With time and her traffic light, she would convince them that she was a scatterbrain no more.

New York City and Its Subways

Millions of people visit New York City every year to see sights such as the Statue of Liberty and Rockefeller Center. But for eight million New Yorkers, this big city is home. Its five boroughs, or political divisions— Manhattan, Brooklyn, Queens, Staten Island, and the Bronx—are divided into neighborhoods.

More than seven hundred miles of subway and elevated train tracks connect these neighborhoods. Laid end to end, the tracks would stretch from New York City to Chicago, Illinois. On October 27, 1904, the Interborough Rapid Transit Subway (IRT) opened the first underground subway line.

Today, 277 of the system's 468 stations are underground. Times Square is the busiest station. Over thirty-five million riders pass through it every year.